We Love Pickup Trucks

by Katherine Lewis

BUMBA BOOKS™

LERNER PUBLICATIONS ◆ MINNEAPOLIS

Note to Educators

Throughout this book, you'll find critical-thinking questions. These can be used to engage young readers in thinking critically about the topic and in using the text and photos to do so.

For Malachi, because trucks are cool!

Lerner Publications Company
An imprint of Lerner Publishing Group, Inc.
241 First Avenue North
Minneapolis, MN 55401 USA

For reading levels and more information, look up this title at www.lernerbooks.com.

Main body text set in Helvetica Textbook Com Roman.
Typeface provided by Linotype AG.

Photo Editor: Cynthia Zemlicka

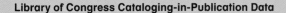

Library of Congress Cataloging-in-Publication Data

Names: Lewis, Katherine, 1996– author.
Title: We love pickup trucks / Katherine Lewis.
Description: Minneapolis : Lerner Publications, [2021] | Series: Bumba books - we love cars and trucks | Includes bibliographical references and index. | Audience: Ages 4–7 | Audience: Grades K–1 | Summary: "Pickup trucks are some of the toughest cars on the road. Learn about different parts of a pickup truck and what makes it the king of the road!"— Provided by publisher.
Identifiers: LCCN 2020019908 (print) | LCCN 2020019909 (ebook) | ISBN 9781728419282 (library binding) | ISBN 9781728420318 (paperback) | ISBN 9781728419305 (ebook)
Subjects: LCSH: Pickup trucks—Juvenile literature.
Classification: LCC TL230.15 .L49 2021 (print) | LCC TL230.15 (ebook) | DDC 629.223/2—dc23

LC record available at https://lccn.loc.gov/2020019908
LC ebook record available at https://lccn.loc.gov/2020019909

Manufactured in the United States of America
1-49044-49260-9/3/2020

Table of Contents

Pickup Trucks

A pickup truck's engine rumbles.

This truck is on the go!

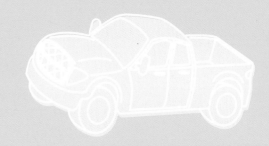

Pickup trucks help

move heavy things.

A driver sits in the cab.

Supplies go in the bed.

A pickup truck has a hitch.

The truck can tow a trailer,

camper, or boat.

What does the hitch help the pickup truck do?

Pickup trucks can tow up to 16,000 pounds (7,257 kg)!

Some pickup truck drivers carry equipment for their jobs.

They might carry logs or heavy tools.

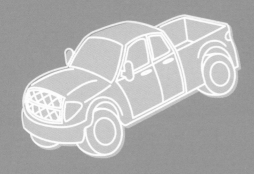

What else might a pickup truck carry?

Pickup trucks are higher off the ground than other cars. Drivers can take their trucks off-road.

When might a driver take a truck off-road?

17

Drivers love their trucks.

They paint them bright colors

and add lights and big tires.

19

A pickup truck will get you

where you need to go!

Parts of a Pickup Truck

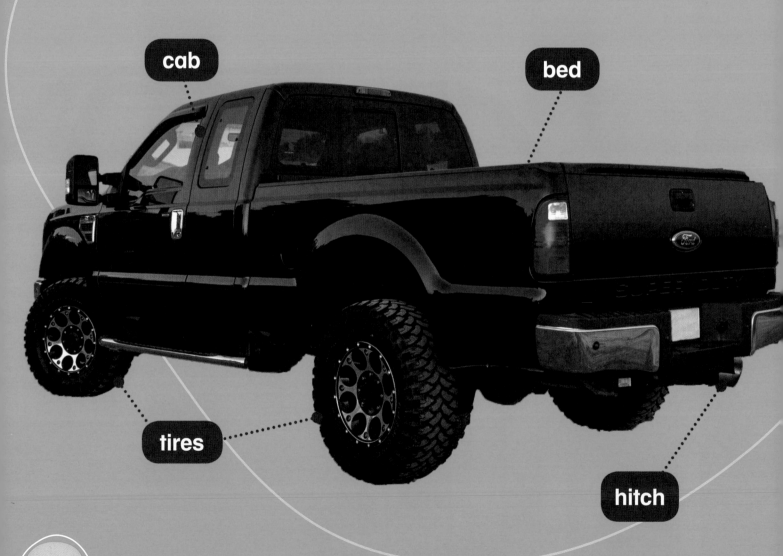

cab

bed

tires

hitch

Picture Glossary

hitch

a tool attached to a truck for towing

off-road

unpaved land or trails

supplies

things you need for a job

trailer

a vehicle or container towed behind a pickup truck

Learn More

Honders, Christine. *Truck Drivers*. New York: PowerKids, 2020.

Kenan, Tessa. *Trucks*. Minneapolis: Jump!, 2018.

Lewis, Katherine. *We Love Sports Cars*. Minneapolis: Lerner Publications, 2021.

Index

Photo Credits